WHO MADE YOU?

BIBLICAL TRUTHS THAT SUPPORT DENOUNCEMENT OF FRATERNITIES, SORORITIES, AND OTHER SECRET SOCIETIES

I0571142

DR. DEANNA MELTON-RIDDLE

www.TrueVinePublishing.org

Who Made You?
Deanna Melton-Riddle

Published by
True Vine Publishing Co
810 Dominican Dr.
Nashville, TN 37228
www.TrueVinePublishing.org

ISBN: 978-1-962783-53-8 Paperback
ISBN: 978-1-962783-54-5 eBook

Scripture quotations marked KJV are taken from the Holy Bible King James Version

ACKNOWLEDGMENTS

I owe total praise and glory to God and His Son, Jesus—my Lord, Savior, and King. The assignment given to me to write this book was an absolute honor and privilege, one I do not take lightly.

To those I know personally, as well as those I do not, who took heed and obeyed the call to denounce your membership, I applaud you for taking a stand. I know it feels uncomfortable at times, but let me encourage you with the same words the Lord led me to, which served as confirmation that I was not alone:

"Trust in the Lord with all thine heart; and lean not unto thine own understanding. In all thy ways acknowledge Him, and He shall direct thy paths." (Proverbs 3:5-6)

I am a witness that God will uphold you and renew you from the inside out. You will see that your obedience was worth it!

TABLE OF CONTENTS

FOREWORD

My purpose in writing this book is, first and foremost, to be obedient to God, led by the Holy Spirit. Secondly, I aim to share the insights God has given me through His Word, enabling others to make informed decisions.

Some readers may feel a sense of release, as they've experienced an inner prompt regarding membership in a fraternity, sorority, or other secret society. Many have wondered if involvement in these organizations aligns with the Word of God. I expect that some will take serious issue with the contents of this book, and I respect everyone's right to choose their own stance.

I am aware that I may come under strong attack for speaking the truth, as "all who live godly in Christ Jesus shall suffer persecution" (2 Timothy 3:12). I understand that truth is not always received in the spirit of love with which it is given. Nevertheless, because I am speaking the truth according to the Word of God, I stand firm in my assignment.

In Christ Jesus,

Dr. Deanna Melton-Riddle

CHAPTER 1

MY INTRODUCTION TO "GREEK LIFE"

G rowing up, I was always involved in my community, participating in organizations such as the NAACP and 4-H Club, and volunteering for various events and causes. However, like many others, I was introduced to the social side of Black fraternity and sorority life (also referred to as "Greek Life") before seeing the public service side.

Before entering college, my older sister attended Alabama State University and would come home during breaks, sharing her experiences with classes, dorm life, and parties where the "Elite Eight" Black Greek letter organizations were heavily represented. While she ultimately didn't pursue membership, our conversations about sororities left a lasting impression on me.

In 1992, during my second year of college, I was invited to a step show that was taking place over summer break when many students were home from college. For those unfamiliar with Black fraternity and sorority life, a step show is an event where each organization is represented by a team of its members who perform "step" routines that are precisely choreographed and rehearsed.

The tradition of step shows in Black fraternities and sororities has roots in African dance and rhythm, reflecting movements and communal expressions found in African cultural heritage. Stepping, as a form of performance, began to take shape in the early to mid-20th century when Black Greek letter organizations embraced it as a unique expression of unity, pride, and identity. Over time, step shows evolved into a signature form of storytelling, celebration, and friendly competition, blending chants, percussive movements, and synchronized dance as a way to acknowledge both the past and the present.

I was thrilled to receive the invitation and decided to attend with a friend who was home from Jackson State University for the summer. As I entered the venue, I was in awe of the strong presence of all eight organizations. Once I found my seat and looked around, I could feel the charged atmosphere, filled with anticipation for each organization's performance. What struck me was the camaraderie on display—not only within each group but also in the genuine, friendly exchanges across organizations.

The whole concept of "Greek Life" was new to me,

as I had never been in circles with many members of these organizations before. The energy of the step show that evening heightened the excitement, with each fraternity and sorority filling the amphitheater with resounding echoes of their unique calls.

By "call," I mean the sound that members use to identify with each other or at parties, representing their organizations. I found myself getting caught up in the excitement of what I was seeing, and before I knew it, I wanted to experience more of what these organizations had to offer—or so I thought.

There are many reasons individuals choose to be part of a fraternity, sorority, or other social and secret societies. Some are genuinely interested in contributing to public and community service efforts on a larger scale. Others join with the expectation that membership will provide valuable "connections" and professional networking opportunities. There are also those who join to "boost" their image and gain popularity, while many are simply seeking a sense of belonging.

Especially within Black Greek letter fraternities and sororities, there is a deep-rooted desire to be part of something that fosters family, togetherness, brotherhood, and sisterhood—things that many people long for. I can

11

say with complete transparency that I identified with more than one of these motivations.

The organization that captured my interest was Delta Sigma Theta Sorority. A very close friend who grew up in my neighborhood had just become a member and she informed me that they were going to have a Rush in the spring of 1993. After further research and getting to know more members of the organization, I decided to attend.

A Rush is an event hosted by a sorority where prospective women interested in membership can learn more about the organization, meet members of the local chapter, and, if they choose, receive an application for membership. Fraternities also hold a similar event for prospective men, called a Smoker. After attending the Rush, I was impressed with what I learned about the organization and the members of the chapter. I decided to submit my application, and shortly after, I was invited to an interview and ultimately accepted as a candidate for membership. By the spring of 1994, I had become a full-fledged member of the organization, with all rights and privileges as designated by the organization's national headquarters.

At the time, it felt like such an honor and accomplishment, but in retrospect, knowing what I know now, these so-called "rights and privileges" came with a price greater than I had bargained for.

CHAPTER 2

THE EXPERIENCE AND TRUTH MEET

F ast forward seven years, and many changes had taken place in my life. The most significant change was my decision to accept Jesus Christ as my Lord and Savior. Although I continued my sorority membership, things began to shift, and I quickly noticed that I felt differently about engaging in certain activities and going to certain places. When I first received salvation, there was such a newness and joy that truly made me feel "born again." As a new believer, I was learning something new each day, and God began to change my desires and appetite for worldly things.

Many things I gave up instantly, but I remained connected to the sorority and maintained close relationships with those who were, at the time, my sorority sisters—especially my line sisters. I vividly recall the first time I felt convicted, on a particular evening when I decided to attend a fraternity party with some of my line sisters. While getting dressed, I immediately felt different from how I had in the past. The excitement I used to feel about representing the organization at parties was no longer there. This was one of many instances where I chose to override the conviction of the Holy Spirit, but once I arrived, it was further confirmed that this was no longer an environment I needed to be in.

As I continued to study the Word, God began to lead me to scripture that was undeniably rhema. I questioned why I was no longer feeling comfortable in settings where I represented the sorority, whether for community service or social gatherings, and the Lord led me to 2 Corinthians 5:17: "Therefore if any man be in Christ, he is a new creature: old things are passed away; behold, all things are become new." Some may try to manipulate this scripture, using the excuse that they were made new from the moment they confessed Jesus as their Lord and Savior, but works must be added to our faith as well. There are no exceptions listed in this scripture; He told us that all things become new, meaning we are not to carry anything associated with the old man and mix it with the new.

There will always be a direct conflict of interest when we try to do so, because the ways of the old man are tied to the lust of the flesh, the lust of the eyes, and the pride of life (1 John 2:16). These characteristics work against the Spirit of God, which operates in righteousness, and trying to mix the two results in a manufactured form of godliness that denies the true power of the Holy Ghost, which comes to set us free from everything connected to our past. No matter how I tried to ignore the tug I was feeling, I couldn't shake it. I soon realized that it was the conviction of the Holy Spirit calling me to separation. I'll discuss the importance and necessity of separation, and what it means in the life of a believer, in a later chapter.

The more I grew in God, the more He began to deal with me and reveal truth through His Holy Spirit. I want to make a point here: there is no such thing as "my truth" or "your truth." If anything we are involved in does not align with God's Word, which is the truth, then it is embedded in deception! If we are honest, many times, out of selfishness and self-will, we choose what we want to accept as the truth and make it our truth.

In 2006, after 12 years in the organization, the Spirit of the Lord arrested me in my living room, and I finally took heed and obeyed. I gathered all my sorority paraphernalia, threw it out, and shredded my membership card and certificate as the Lord instructed me to do. I didn't fully understand why God told me to do it; I just knew I heard His voice, and I was moved to obey.

As I purged my room and my house of everything related to the sorority, I briefly considered passing some items on to those still in the organization. But I vividly remember the Holy Ghost speaking to me, saying, "No: if I am setting you free, why would you give it to someone else and serve as a stumbling block?" Understand, ultimately it is each individual's decision to remain and stay connected to the organization, but when you have received knowledge and instruction from God to separate from something, you are then charged with the responsibility to serve as an example and inform others. I didn't question God; I simply humbled myself and obeyed.

CHAPTER 3

WHY THE CHANGE?

In the early years of my walk with Christ, I served within the Church of God in Christ. In addition to my upbringing in the Pentecostal holiness church, which I now serve and lead under, I thank God for the teachings I received while being a part of COGIC, which taught me how to walk in truth, holiness, and righteousness. During this time, I recall different pastors and evangelists preaching against membership in fraternities and sororities, though they never fully explained why.

I want to reiterate a point I previously made: the more I grew in God—through prayer, seeking Him, meditating on His Word, and fasting—my relationship with Him strengthened, and I became more attentive to and led by His Holy Spirit. We must remember that the Holy Spirit (or Holy Ghost) "teaches us all things and brings all things to our remembrance" according to John 14:26. What began to happen was that the Holy Ghost was reminding me of what I read in the Word of God, giving me divine revelation and enlightening my understanding of what was expected of me. The Spirit of God came on strongly, and I could not shake it; He began to lead me to more scriptures, such as, "Come out from among them and be ye separate, saith the Lord" (2 Corinthians 6:17).

Now, many may read this and say, "I know that I have a relationship with God, I have served him faithfully for years and I know His voice; what He says to you is not what He said to me."

Well, my answer is that while God absolutely has different paths for us individually in our walk of salvation, He is certainly not the author of confusion. When it comes to His divine instructions and commandments for His people to live righteous and holy lives, He is very clear when He speaks. Like so many others that God has spoken to, I simply chose to obey and no longer make provision for my flesh and what it wanted.

Many will not admit it, and may even downplay it, but there is a soul tie that develops through the bonding process, which causes you to become connected to the organization and those who are a part of it.

A soul tie is defined as: A metaphysical connection between a person and someone or something else, formed by being extremely close to them.

The power of soul ties keeps a person connected through relationships, the bonds formed, and the habitual practice of certain activities that are part of the organizational culture. This is what prompts such a strong reaction of anger and resistance when truth begins to be revealed through the Word of God. The Bible clearly tells us that "the flesh lusteth against the spirit, and the spirit against the flesh, and these are contrary one to the other: so that ye cannot do the things that ye would" (Galatians 5:17). In the flesh, we are concerned about the bonds that have been created and the years invested in the organization, which interferes with one's willingness to hear and obey the leading of the Spirit of God. The flesh will always defend and fight for what it wants, because there is no good thing in it, according to Romans 7:18.

Let's delve into the many reasons why God is against membership in Black Greek-letter organizations and other secret societies, and why I chose to obey and denounce my membership.

Are You Sure It Was God?

Let's address the negative feedback and accusations that will inevitably come: first, I have no desire to be seen or to draw attention to myself, nor did anyone "offend me." I clearly heard from the Lord regarding His displeasure with my involvement in Delta Sigma Theta Sorority, and yes, I chose to obey when He dealt with me to make a decision to separate. I've heard many say, "No denouncement over here; I'm good," and if that is your stance, you are within your right to choose.

But I would encourage you to remember the instruction of the Lord to the children of Israel in Deuteronomy 30:19: "I call heaven and earth to record this day against you, that I have set before you life and death, blessing and cursing: therefore choose life, that both thou and thy seed may live."

The choice of life comes with making the decision to obey God when He calls us to separation. Before I got to the place of total submission and obedience, there were several instances where the Lord was dealing with me about separation, and like many, I would discount that I was hearing from God.

After all, it is a fact that the premise of what is now known as the Divine Nine organizations is that they were "founded on Christian principles and beliefs." This statement has served as a point of deception, because founding members of each of these organizations had ties to the church. In fact, to claim the title "Divine" does not align with its true meaning. The word "divine" is associated with *"that which pertains to God; eternal, holy; related to divinity or theology."*

It is important that I make this statement: I have no doubt that the founders had good intentions and truly believed they were laying a Christ-like foundation. In our human frame, we believe that we know what is best and that God supports every decision we make, but the Bible is clear that "our ways are not His ways and our thoughts are not His thoughts" (Isaiah 55:8).

The scripture rings true that "there is a way that seemeth right unto man, but the end thereof are the ways of death" (Proverbs 14:12). It may have seemed right to incorporate scripture into the rituals and substitute words that point directly to the representation of the organization, but God told us that He would not give His glory to another. "Death and life are in the power of the tongue, and they that love it shall eat the fruit thereof" (Proverbs 18:21). When one willingly recites various chants and vows and takes part in the organization's ritualistic ceremonies, they are partaking of deadly fruit. "Whatsoever we do in word and deed must be done as unto the Lord," according to Colossians 3:17.

Everyone who is still involved in these organizations must be completely honest with themselves and ask the question: Is every deed that I do and every word that comes out of my mouth as a part of this organization pleasing and can be presented holy and acceptable unto the Lord, which is my reasonable service according to Romans 12:2?

I can recall when I was a part of the organization, anytime we attended the wedding of a sorority sister, we would sing what is known as the Sweetheart Song. There is a certain part of the song that says,

"She may be an Omega sweetheart, or the dream girl of A-phi-A, she may wear the Kappa's diamond, or her love may a Sigma be, but if she wears the Delta symbol, then her first love is DST."

Of course, this has been and will continue to be defended by statements such as, "These are just words, I would never put my organization before God." But does not the Bible tell us that "out of the abundance of the heart, the mouth speaketh" (Matthew 12:34)?

To say that Delta is your first love suggests that something has taken the place that only God should occupy. In Revelation 2:4, God spoke directly to the church of Ephesus and said, "I have somewhat against you because you have left your first love." What He was saying was that they had come to a place where the affection, attention, and time set aside for God was now being given to other things. The argument is always, "These are just words to a song, they don't mean anything to me." However, we must be reminded of the words that Jesus spoke to the Pharisees in Matthew 12:34: "O generation of vipers, how can ye, being evil, speak good things? For out of the abundance of the heart the mouth speaketh."

Now, on the other side of the coin, we must ask ourselves: How can we, who declare that we are "good" Christians, speak evil things that contradict the commandments of God? Because of the connection between the heart and the words that we speak, we should never speak words out of our mouth that we don't mean or believe.

MINERVA

I will never forget when I was contacted by the representative chapter in my region to finalize my separation from the sorority. I received a call from the Chaplain, which I knew would begin with an attempt to try and "reclaim" me as a member. One of the first things she said to me was, "You know, once you make this decision, it can't be reversed," and my reply was, "I am aware." Here is a word of encouragement to those who are in a place of decision: when you know that God is leading you to separate, obey quickly and don't allow the ungodly and unwise counsel of man to cause you to second guess.

The second statement concerned me deeply and further confirmed why the Lord was calling me out of the organization when she said, "You know, we may say Minerva, but we don't worship her." For clarity, Minerva is a Greek goddess, who is said to have been great in power in the areas of music, medicine, arts and crafts, and great wisdom. Her so-called "wisdom" is what Delta Sigma Theta recognizes her for, and thus she is displayed on the sorority's crest. Within myself, I said, "Did she just say that? Did she just admit that the members of the organization acknowledge a false and idol god in their rituals, but they don't worship her?" This is in direct opposition to the Father, as He is and should be given His rightful glory as "the only wise God" (1 Timothy 1:17; Romans 16:27; Jude 1:25).

I was also reminded of the words that David sang in the 19th Psalm, verse 14: "Let the words of my mouth, and the meditation of my heart, be acceptable in thy sight, O LORD, my strength and my redeemer." How could one ever think that acknowledging an idol goddess would ever be acceptable in the sight of the Lord? The spirit of deception puts up a front that highlights public service, sisterhood and brotherhood, but behind that front lies the truths that have to do with hazing, the rituals, the chants, the vows, the partying, and the paraphernalia that is worn.

For those who say that I am taking this too far and making something out of nothing, I say to you that I am taking this as far as the spirit of the Lord leads me to go. Everything that has to do with this world carries a spirit, whether good or evil.

One of the mandates that God Himself set forth and made very clear is found in John 4:24: "God is a Spirit: and they that worship Him must worship Him in spirit and in truth." To worship God is to honor and respect Him, and doing so in spirit and in truth means that we are led, governed, and influenced by the Holy Spirit, which causes us to acknowledge and obey God's commands and not conform to the desires of our flesh.

To devote space in our dwelling, whether it be in our homes, on our cars, or on our bodies, to represent the organizations by wearing clothing that bears shields and crests with idol gods and goddesses is, in fact, disrespectful to God the Father. Make no mistake, membership in these organizations carries a strongman of temptation, and once you are in, you become linked to strongholds that will keep you bound for as long as you allow.

For a better understanding of these two key words, let's look at the definitions as they pertain to these organizations:

* **Strongman** – a forceful or brutal person, usually a ruler or tyrant.

* **Stronghold** – a place of domination by, or refuge or survival of, a particular group.

So, when you take these definitions at face value, it reveals the level of strong influence that can literally take over and rule one's decision-making, thought process, and behavior. As I stated before, many members of these organizations find comfort in and cherish the bonds and relationships that have been built over time, which makes it more difficult to separate the longer time passes by.

THE SPIRIT OF ALLEGIANCE

So many saints of God at large joined a fraternity or

sorority as an undergraduate or graduate student prior to giving their life to the Lord. Some were raised in the church and knew that membership in these organizations was forbidden, but the atmosphere on college campuses breeds a level of enticement that can be very persuasive.

By definition, allegiance means: fidelity, adherence, loyalty. When one holds allegiance to someone or something, they show reverence and loyalty. This loyal and reverent mannerism is displayed through comments that come against those who have taken a stand to denounce their membership. The level of anger and ungodly disposition that has been seen by those who profess to be Christians is quite concerning—many hold positions in the church as pastors and bishops.

For many, this allegiance to the cause of their respective organizations has crept in and turned them over to the spirits of pride and arrogance. There is a word of caution that we all should be reminded of, which is found in Proverbs 16:18: "Pride goeth before destruction and an haughty spirit before a great fall." No one, and I mean no one, is exempt from the judgments of God.

CHAPTER 4

WHO MADE YOU?

I need to further explain the context of the question "Who Made You?", which is the reason that God impressed upon me to write this book. Once an individual has been accepted for membership, they begin what is known as the pledge process. This process looks different for many, depending on who is involved, whether at the undergraduate or graduate level.

The "formal" and legal process, as set forth by National Headquarters, involves initiate members, also known as pledgees, taking part in a series of different rituals where they learn about the origins of the organization, what it stands for, and the expectations once they are members. They are taught by members of the organization who serve in that chapter.

In contrast, there is another process that occurs, referred to as going "underground," where the illegal activities of hazing take place. It has been recorded that as early as the 1930s, the practice of hazing found its way into the process of fraternity and sorority membership initiations. Although I speak from the perspective of Black Greek letter organizations, let me be clear that this practice is just as prevalent in white fraternities and sororities. However, the significance of hazing within black fraternities and sororities carries a different meaning, as it is supposed to serve as a way to ensure that pledgees or initiates on a particular line "bond" with one another and learn humility.

There are "big sisters" who oversee the pledge process, to whom the pledgees must answer and respond to any requests that they make. Pledgees are also considered to be a "lower" extension of the organization's symbolism. For example, as a pledgee on the line for Delta Sigma Theta, I was acknowledged as Pyramid Deanna and had an assigned number according to my position on the line. The physical, mental, and emotional abuse inflicted upon pledgees is supposed to serve as a means of identifying with the suffering that our ancestors experienced and the demeaning acts that they were subjected to during slavery.

This entire process is known as pledging, and the activities that take place during the pledge process are referred to as "being made." When someone makes a pledge, they are actually making a solemn promise to be committed to whatever is asked or required of them. Once the revelation of this truth became real, I also began to see other areas in my life where a denouncement needed to take place, and this is why I no longer participate in "pledging allegiance" to the United States flag. I can show respect and appreciation for those who serve our country without pledging allegiance to a flag.

Thinking in retrospect, and now having the wisdom and knowledge of the Holy Ghost, I also understand just how foolish it was to ever think that any manmade process could ever serve as any type of example of what our ancestors suffered and endured as slaves. To say that one was "made" is likened to a badge of honor, so to speak. When one is known as being "made," it supposedly certifies you as being "real," having gone through a process that is respected, as opposed to being what is known as "paper."

The reference to being "paper" means that an individual only went through the ceremonial rituals where all members and advisors of the chapter were present. The definition of "made" means to "produce, manufacture by constructing, shaping, or forming." Man's making is a false representation of a function that only God can do.

John 1:3 states, "All things were made by him; and without him was not anything made that was made." So, to even suggest or make the statement that you have "made" someone is an insult to God. "God created man in his own image, in the image of God created he him" (Genesis 1:27).

Know this: man never has and never will have the power to remake something that God has already made! Just to make things very clear, this in no way includes the life that is produced by way of a man and woman coming together, resulting in the birth of a child, which still originates from the order that God set in place in the beginning.

As we yet live and walk in our salvation, we are being made and molded daily to model godly character, which can only be done through the spirit of God, not man. How insulting it is to state the claim that we have made someone when God clearly tells us that he formed us from our mother's womb. It insinuates that we needed to redo God's work: it is a contradiction and an attempt to take God's glory, which He says that He will not give to another. While it is understood that there is a level of humility and respect for mankind that we all must have and should be subject to some means of authority here on earth, we are only to come under God's complete rule and subjection. Only the spirit of God can teach us true humility.

Again, I believe that the founders meant well when laying out the plans for these organizations and choosing the Greek letters that would represent their organizations, but there is a line that is crossed when one identifies or acknowledges a position that only God holds. The word of God clearly states that He is "Alpha and Omega, the beginning and the end." There is a danger that comes with taking on this same position as a man: it presents as a false representation and form of exaltation of oneself, which is the reason that the devil was kicked out of heaven.

To declare any being or entity as being Alpha or Omega is a form of taking God's glory, according to Isaiah 42:8. This doesn't only refer to a few, but there is a tendency for members of all organizations to identify themselves by stating, "I am a Delta," or "I am an AKA," or "I am a Sigma." There is a difference in someone say-ing "I am a Delta" vs. "I am a member of Delta Sigma Theta Sorority," because one insinuates that you are a direct extension of the organization.

Think about it this way: I identify myself as a

"Christian," which makes me an extension of Christ Jesus, because it is through the shedding of his blood that he redeemed my life from sin, and I became an heir to the throne of the kingdom of heaven and a joint heir with Christ.

I recall one particular evening during our pyramid induction ceremony when the big sisters were teaching us about the Codes of Conduct, so to speak, and how we must represent the sorority. One of the points they talked about was refraining from going out in public wearing hair rollers with any sorority paraphernalia on.

Quite frankly, there should be a standard of appropriate dress code when we go out in public, just because it is proper. However, I thought about the fact that we should never be more concerned about adhering to the mandates and protocols that dictate how we should present ourselves in public because we "represent" a man-made organization, more than we are mindful of being heedful to the word of God, which mandates how we are to represent the kingdom of God as born-again believers on a daily basis.

Willfully Worshiping Idols

For many, one of the most rewarding experiences of

becoming a member of a fraternity or sorority (especially as a neophyte/neo, which is a new member) is to be presented with paraphernalia that bears the letters and symbols of the organization. Members who represent each of the organizations under what is known as the Divine Nine can be seen wearing items such as t-shirts, sweatshirts, buttons, pins, hats, jackets, and even bags. The problem that lies within such representation is the symbolism behind what is being displayed. Idolatry occurs when there is manipulation to fit a desired preference or appetite. We choose to follow that which "appeals" to our lives and displays certain characteristics that we want to identify with. This is what causes individuals to identify with and choose what organizations they want to be a part of.

Here is what I mean by the subtitle "Willfully Worshiping Idols":

- Willful – intentional; deliberate; stubborn and determined.

- Idol – a graven image or representation of something that is revered, or believed to convey spiritual power;

- Revere – to respect or give reverence. An act of showing respect, such as a bow.

Here is something to ponder: how many times have I bowed during a ceremony or ritual, the way that I should only bow in prayer or in worship to acknowledge the Lord? How often do I repetitively recite mantras and vows, where I manipulate scripture to replace words with the name of the organization? How often do I willfully participate in chants about my love and devotion to the organization?

In the past, I attended the funerals of people who were a part of not only fraternities and sororities, but also masons and eastern stars, where they were dressed in and covered in paraphernalia in the form of sashes and pins. I watched as people were literally throwing shirts and pinning buttons and other items representing the organization into their caskets. The fraternity and sorority chapters of the respective state of the deceased members are allowed to conduct ceremonies as part of the funeral service, where they acknowledge that the deceased member is now a part of the Omega, Omega chapter, signifying the end.

Consider the context of this: the organization has taken on an act of "confirming" this soul into a final destination. As petty as this may seem to many, it is actually a contradiction to God's order, which has designated two places for mankind when they leave this earth: they will either live eternally with Him in heaven if they lived a sanctified and holy life, or in hell if they refused to depart from a life of sin and disobedience.

I refer back to my previously stated point that God established His identity from the beginning as Alpha and Omega, so it is impossible for man to claim that when someone passes away, they are now a part of another chapter, where they now have "eternal" membership.

PARAPHERNALIA SYMBOLISM

I mentioned in previous chapters that the founders of Black Greek letter organizations prefaced that their foundations were built on Christian principles and beliefs. However, a great contradiction exists when the symbolisms of the organizations are those of Greek gods and goddesses. This is a prime example of what Paul mentioned in II Timothy 3:5 when he warned Timothy, stating that "in the last days, men would have a form of godliness, denying the power thereof: from such turn away."

How is this scripture relevant, you may ask? One of the first arguments that those who are in the church bring forth when challenged on membership is the reference to Christian principles, which serves as their point of justification. But the objects that represent these organizations bear symbolisms that are in contradiction to what believers should be associated with.

All fraternities and sororities have a crest or shield, each with a different meaning for the organization; but what they all have in common is a picture of a Greek god or goddess who represents a particular characteristic that the organization acknowledges. We cannot wear the name of Christ and wear Minerva or any other false god. How does one wear these idol gods? By willingly purchasing and accepting clothing or any other items that bear their picture.

GRAVEN IMAGES

The carving of wooden paddles with the Greek letters of the organization is not only displayed in homes by hanging on walls and being placed upon shelves (which serves as a form of idol worship) but is also used in hazing activities to "discipline" pledgees. The Bible is clear about God's displeasure with the carving of graven images that were used for idolatry. I refer back to Isaiah 42:8: "I am the LORD: that is my name: my glory will I not give to another, neither my praise to graven images."

In the book of Acts 19, beginning at verse 23, the

Apostle Paul was charged with the assignment of warning the people of Ephesus, which was the capital of Asia, about their idol worship practices. There was a man by the name of Demetrius who made a living as a silversmith: a silversmith is someone who is able to make crafts out of silver, such as jewelry.

The problem was that he was making the jewelry for the people to present as worship to the goddess Diana. Diana was the idol that the Ephesians acknowledged as their god, and she was crafted and created by man to represent fertility. Notice the sharp rebuke that Paul gave to the Ephesians as stated by Demetrius: "Moreover ye see and hear, that not alone at Ephesus, but almost throughout all Asia, this Paul hath persuaded and turned away much people, saying that they be no gods, which are made with hands: so that not only this our craft is in danger to be set at nought, but also that the temple of the great goddess Diana should be despised, and her magnificence should be destroyed."

Some may argue that this has no relevance because we are not worshiping idols or gods, just as the regional Chaplain expressed to me. However, the fact that one willfully associates with what these images represent shows acceptance and agreement. Remember the words of Amos 3:3: "Can two walk together, except they be agreed?" Not only should those who purchase these items be warned, but those who make and craft such things that they ultimately sell for profit. The carving of wooden paddles, the making of jackets, and windbreakers are subject to the same warning as Paul gave Demetrius.

Notice also that Paul urged them to destroy the temple where the idol god was kept: any place that is used to house any idol representation, whether it be in the home, in an automobile, in a sorority or fraternity house, or at the office of headquarters, is subject to the mandate that Paul issued.

Regardless of the fact that these places are not sanctuaries, they serve as houses of "worship" due to the false deities that are acknowledged and housed within.

RITUALS

One of the most practiced activities that has to do with membership in sororities, fraternities, and other secret-letter societies is participation in rituals. A ritual is a set of actions that one carries out repeatedly, which is what happens during membership intake ceremonies, chapter meetings, regional and national conventions. It is in these types of settings where the scripture "having a form of godliness, denying the power thereof" can truly be seen.

While there is an assigned Chaplain who serves the purpose of opening up the organization's business activities with prayer, there are ceremonial practices carried out that require the reciting of oaths directed toward one's commitment to the organization. Zechariah 8:17 specifically speaks to God's displeasure and forbidding of false oaths. An oath is a solemn pledge or promise, so if one's argument is that they don't really mean what they are saying, then it is still considered an error because it is out of alignment with God's requirement to obey only His commandments.

Another ritualistic practice that takes place during underground hazing activities is what is known as a "death march." During the death march, pledgees are subjected to more intense hazing to challenge their endurance and ability to trust one another and stick together under pressure. I recall one experience while on line, where we each had duffle bags that were to contain fifteen large rocks, representing the number of people on our line at that time.

One particular evening, I needed to lend mine to one

of my line sisters. She was not able to continue with our line, which left me without rocks, and I was not able to obtain any more in time for the death march. Out of desperation and fear, I put a Bible into my bag, and we hoped that none of the big sisters would check my bag. Well, it just so happened that our Dean of Pledges (the one who was the overseer of our line) checked my bag and got furious, throwing it in the water with my Bible inside! She then turned to me and said, "This is not the place for religion."

Little did I realize at the time that she could not have made a more true statement. It is important to understand what "death" represents:

The cessation of life and all associated processes; the end of an organism's existence as an entity independent from its environment and its return to a nonliving state; the collapse or end of something; spiritual lifelessness.

Jesus came to save us and give us more abundant life according to John 10:10; so why would anyone subject themselves to something that threatens to leave them "spiritually lifeless"? Looking at the context of what it truly means when the process of death is taking place, I can clearly see now that this act served no purpose in the natural, and certainly not in the spirit. Not only was that not the place for religion, but there was no place for justification of how God could be glorified as a result of what was taking place.

SONGS AND CHANTS

The songs and chants that are recited in honor of the organization, where people profess a love so strong that they would climb the highest mountain or swim the deepest ocean and even die for it! (As much as I hate to admit it, this is a song that I used to sing.) Is this not a form of worship and idolatry, where one is idly worshiping an idol with their mouth? The songs and ceremonies that happen to mention God are not received by God as we would like to think.

Here is what God has to say about such "forms" of godliness:

"I hate, I despise your feast days, and I will not smell in your solemn assemblies. Though ye offer me burnt offerings and your meat offerings, I will not accept them: neither will I regard the peace offerings of your fat beasts. Take away from me the noise of thy songs; for I will not hear the melody of thy viols. But let judgment run down as waters, and righteousness as a mighty stream." —Amos 5:21-24

God was speaking through the prophet Amos to the Israelites about the false worship that they were rendering to God. He did not receive their worship because what they were speaking out of their mouths did not align with their actions. As I mentioned in a previous chapter, we must keep in mind that God's ways are not our ways, and His thoughts are not our thoughts (Isaiah 55:8). Just because we believe something to be acceptable to God doesn't mean that it is.

How do we know what is acceptable to God? I refer back to the following the blueprint set forth by the Apostle Paul in Romans 12:1, which states:

"I beseech ye therefore, brethren, by the mercies of God, that ye present your bodies a living sacrifice, holy, acceptable unto God, which is your reasonable service."

One sure way to find out if what you are involved in is acceptable by God's standards is to weigh it in the spirit and check the holiness gauge!

BRANDING AND TATTOOS

Another ritual that found its way into the culture of Black Greek letter organizations is that of branding. Let's first look at where the process of branding derived from: it is used as a means of identifying cattle who are roaming on ranges and, if they happened to stray away, they could be returned to their owners. The danger of just simply adapting to so-called "norms" of what is acceptable by society's standards is that it will more than likely conflict with Godly standards.

Think about it: allowing someone to brand your body with the letters or any symbol of an organization in essence represents ownership. Why is this a conflict? If you profess to be a saint of God, then you know that God says that "all souls are mine" (Ezekiel 18:4). We also cannot ignore Leviticus 19:28, which states:

"Ye shall not make any cuttings in your flesh for the dead, nor print any marks upon you: I am the Lord."

The reference to not making any cuttings in the flesh for the dead speaks to tattoos or any marking on one's body that pay tribute or remembrance to someone who has passed on. This also speaks to the forbiddance of any such tattoos and branding on the body that show reverence to a person or thing, such as an organization, which is simply another form of idol worship.

Let me be clear: if someone received a brand or tattoo prior to receiving Christ as their Lord and Savior, then that sin was forgiven when you repented. However, to willingly continue to subject your body to markings of any kind after being made aware of and acknowledging the requirements of godly and righteous living is unpleasing to God.

Do we not use our hands to worship and war in the spirit, by lifting our hands unto God and the clapping of our hands to usher in His presence and give Him praise and glory? So how then can we take those same hands and render signs to acknowledge an organization that is clothed in idolatry?

These same hands have also been used to create and swing the same wooden paddles that bear idol images on pledgees. Again, I say, while you may not physically serve the idol god, you hold allegiance to something that acknowledges the idol, which shows agreement and fellowship. In the book of 2 Corinthians 6:14, Paul was speaking to the Corinthians and warned them of things to avoid as Christians:

"Be ye not unequally yoked with unbelievers: for what fellowship hath righteousness with unrighteousness? And what communion hath light with darkness? And what concord hath Christ with Belial? Or what part hath he that believeth with an infidel? And what agreement hath the temple of God with idols? For ye are the temple of the living God." These deeds come before the Lord as works that will be judged and tried by fire according to Jeremiah 25:4-7.

CHAPTER 5

WHY DENOUNCE?

I t is important to establish what it means to denounce:

Denounce – To make known in a formal manner; to proclaim; to announce; to declare.

There will be many who, from the moment they begin reading this book, will find it serves as immediate confirmation that the Lord has been dealing with them about denouncement. It is for this reason that God has summoned so many to make public statements when they have made the decision to denounce their organizations. It is one thing to simply say that you no longer want to be involved in the organization; it may even be followed by refraining from attending gatherings or meetings. But God requires commitment—action that shows we mean what we say and that we honor and obey His request to "come out from among them and be separate, saith the Lord."

It is necessary to reiterate that to those who say, "God didn't tell me that," it may not be that God hasn't tried to get your attention, but rather that you have chosen to block out what He said because it is uncomfortable. You have a right to choose to stay in the place where you are, as God has given us all the right to choose. What we don't have the right to do is demean or try to discredit others who make the choice to obey God.

Instead of defending the organization, we should be defending the truth of the gospel and earnestly contending for the faith, as servants of God who are called according to His purpose. As saints of God, we are automatically called to a life of servanthood, and there are no boundaries within that calling. There will always be a need and opportunity to serve internationally, nationally, locally, and within our respective individual and church communities until Jesus returns. That means we are free to serve within our community, outside of our community, on the mission field, and beyond, without having to be tied to an organization.

As members of the body of Christ, we have brothers and sisters in Christ. Regardless of the actions of some who, at times, don't display brotherly or sisterly love, it doesn't speak for the body as a whole.

What distinguishes membership in the body of Christ from other memberships is that the establishment of the body is built on a sure foundation, where the principles are tried and true, without fault or fail, without hidden agendas and impurities, without yokes or bondages, or any ungodly or unholy connections. I feel impressed to pause again and say that the Word of God speaks clearly, but we don't always like what it has to say when it draws us out of our comfort zones and challenges us to change. Many of those whom the Lord has reached are being led to cry aloud and spare not, and as a result, they are coming under strong attacks, especially from those who profess to be sanctified.

Let me encourage those of you who are taking a stand to do as Jesus told His disciples in Luke 10:10: "But into whatsoever city ye enter, and they receive you not, go your ways out into the streets of the same, and say, Even the very dust of your city, which cleaveth on us, we do wipe off against you: notwithstanding, be ye sure of this, that the kingdom of God is come nigh unto you."

I refer back to the definition of what it means to denounce, which includes two words that are key: proclaim and announce, which only confirms the necessity of making it public. Everyone will not receive the message and call to denounce if their heart hasn't been broken to a place of total humility. But one thing that is sure, in the end, the truth concerning this matter will speak.

CHAPTER 6

PRESERVING GENERATIONS

This call to separation is far more critical than many are willing to acknowledge, and it is a trick of the enemy to infiltrate bloodlines by building legacies. A legacy is established when members of the same family become a part of the same organization: for example, a mother and daughter, father and son, sisters, or brothers. Especially in Black Greek-letter organizations, families take great pride in seeing their loved ones join allegiance with their organization of choice; it serves as another extension of bonding.

It is the emotional expression of tears of joy and the excitement of traditions that are passed down that have deceived so many over the years. Some families may not have established a legacy but have generations of family members who are a part of different Black Greek-letter organizations and other secret societies. From a carnal perspective, entering the "Divine Nine" is seen as an honor to be celebrated, but many fail to see what lies in wait in the spirit to take captive your sons, daughters, and other loved ones.

The level of spiritual bondage is likened to what the prophet Ezekiel described:

"Wherefore say unto the house of Israel, Thus saith the Lord GOD; Are ye polluted after the manner of your fathers? And commit ye whoredom after their abominations? For when ye offer your gifts, when ye make your sons pass through the fire, ye pollute yourselves with all your idols, even unto this day: and shall I be enquired of you, O house of Israel? As I live, saith the Lord GOD, I will not be enquired of by you. And that which cometh into your mind shall not be at all, that ye say, We will be as the heathen, as the families of the countries, to serve wood and stone." (Ezekiel 20:30-32)

When sons, daughters, and other members of our families are encouraged to join these organizations to keep a legacy or tradition alive, it literally sets the stage for a generational curse. This was a category that I fell into, as my father pledged when he was in college and sadly died still being affiliated. I thank God that He extended His mercy toward me and allowed me to cut off the generational curse, sparing my son from the ungodly bondages and soul ties within these organizations.

This is exactly what God is doing in this last and final hour before the return of Jesus, sending out a clarion call: a call to separation for His sons and daughters. The enemy is also using his cunning and crafty ways to lure the people of God into honorary membership status. Those who are granted honorary membership in a sorority or fraternity are exempt from going through the initiation process that undergraduates and graduates are subject to. Although they don't go through the same processes, once they accept membership, they have made the decision to come into agreement with what the organization represents.

However, it is no surprise, because Paul warned us in Colossians 2:8 when he stated: "Beware lest any man spoil you through philosophy and vain deceit, after the tradition of men, after the rudiments of the world, and not after Christ."

The false presentation of an organization that upholds godly principles while also acknowledging idol gods has lured members of the body of Christ. Holding a "church service" or hosting an event where "gospel artists" perform isn't wrong, but it also doesn't align with the grounds on which the organization stands.

If we become new creatures in Christ, and "old things are passed away, and all things become new," then why connect with things that threaten to taint the new man?

The Spirit of God led me to the book of Exodus 34:12-16, to remind me of the stern warning that God spoke through Moses to the children of Israel. He warned them not to make any such covenant or show of joining together with any of the enemies in the lands that God was destroying because of their idol worship. Here is what He told them:

"Take heed to thyself, lest thou make a covenant with the inhabitants of the land whither thou goest, lest it be for a snare in the midst of thee: but ye shall destroy their altars, break their images, and cut down their groves: for thou shalt worship no other god; for the Lord, whose name is Jealous, is a jealous God: lest thou make a covenant with the inhabitants of the land, and they go a whoring after their gods, and do sacrifice unto their gods, and one call thee, and go a whoring after their gods, and make thy sons go a whoring after their gods." (Exodus 34:12-16)

To understand the relevancy of this scripture, keep in mind what God had done for the children of Israel, as

Solomon recalled in his prayer in I Kings 9:53:

"For thou didst separate them from among all the people of the earth, to be Thine inheritance, as Thou spakest by the hand of Moses Thy servant, when Thou broughtest our fathers out of Egypt, O Lord God."

Again, we know that God gave these specific instructions to the children of Israel not to follow the customs, practices, and traditions of others around them who served other gods. These commandments still stand for God's people today. Because of the yokes of bondage that were broken off our lives and the deliverance from sins that had us bound, we are to refrain from anything that threatens to entangle us again with the yoke of bondage. God gave them three instructions that they were to act upon:

1. Destroy their altars
2. Break their images
3. Cut down their groves

This is powerful because of what each of these monuments represents when you look at their definitions:

* Altar – a table or flat-topped structure used for religious rites
* Image – a statue or idol
* Grove – a lodge or place of worship

So, in essence, they were gathering together in a designated place for the purpose of showing reverence (recall the definition of an idol in Chapter 4) by participating in acts of religious rites of passage and customs. Sound familiar? It should, because this is exactly what takes place when ceremonies are held during national conventions, chapter meetings, and induction ceremonies for new initiates.

Notice the consequences of what Moses said would happen if the children of Israel disobeyed and began to take on the customs and practices of those around them who engaged in forms of idolatry. Their disobedience did not just affect those who committed such acts, but it had a domino effect on their bloodlines.

CHAPTER 7

GOD IS SPEAKING:
THE CALL TO SEPARATION

I understood from the moment that God assigned me to write this book that it would not be received by all. Because of the love that has grown in the hearts of many who serve within their respective organizations, many see the topic of separating from them as an attack. Specifically, because of the deep roots that lie within the reasons these organizations were founded, it is clearly understood that the basis for Black Greek-letter organizations being established was to create a sense of community for Black people. During a time when we were seen as unvaluable and irrelevant, these organizations provided Black men and women with a sense of belonging and dignity.

God loves His people; He knows that in our human frame, there is a tendency to cling to those things that we become familiar with and develop ties to. Because He is so merciful and compassionate, He extends His mercy to give us a chance to get in order.

This book is not for those who take issue with the fact that God is calling His people to publicly denounce their memberships, but it is for those who have a heart and mind that are set and sensitive to hear, as stated in Revelation 2:29: "He that hath an ear, let him hear what the Spirit saith unto the churches."

While some may have denounced their membership because of personal reasons and disappointments, many denouncements have come by way of God dealing with people. These are the ones who possess a broken spirit and a broken and contrite heart, willing to submit to the leading of the Spirit of God, even when initially they don't like it or don't completely understand why.

Here is what it all boils down to: the contents of this book were not written as a source for debate. It was God-instructed, in accordance with His Word, and those who read it will either accept it or reject it. Please be aware of this fact: once truth has been revealed to us as believers, we are then held accountable based on what we know. I know for many, there is a fear associated with making the decision to leave something so familiar, with so many relationships tied to it.

I've been there. I know what it feels like to go

through a period where you feel alone because, for 10 years or more, all you knew as your circle of friends were your line/sorority sisters or your line/fraternity brothers. There were times when I would sit and reminisce about the times we laughed, talked, and came together to support one another. Please understand that there were good memories I shared with members of the organization; unfortunately, it is the underlying connections within the organization that displease God. But what I also know is that "God hath not given us the spirit of fear; but of power, and of love, and of a sound mind" (2 Timothy 1:7). Anything that God requires us to separate from is because it is not profitable for our spiritual growth. More importantly, ungodly connections such as this jeopardize one's position in obtaining eternal life.

There is a direct message and warning for the people of God that was delivered through song by Asaph in Psalm 81:8-16 that should not be ignored. Beginning at verse 8, the words are as follows:

"Hear, O my people, and I will testify unto thee: O Israel, if thou wilt hearken unto me; There shall no strange god be in thee; Neither shalt thou worship any strange god, I am the

LORD thy God, which brought thee out of the land of Egypt; Open thy mouth wide, and I will fill it. But my people would not hearken to my voice; And Israel would none of me. So I gave them up unto their own heart's lust: And they walked in their own counsels. Oh that my people had hearkened unto me, And Israel had walked in my ways! I should soon have subdued their enemies, And turned my hand against their adversaries. The haters of the Lord should have submitted themselves unto him..."

These verses are pertinent because they describe the willing disobedience of those who were identified as the children of God. We can clearly see in verses 8-10 how God extended mercy, grace, favor, and divine provision for them continually. When we get to verse 11, it is then that God begins to point out the ways of the children of Israel that displeased Him. He also lays out the severe consequences that they suffered: the children of Israel were repeatedly warned to turn from their wicked and sinful acts.

Unfortunately, as a result of their disobedience and the choice they made to continually ignore His instructions and commandments, God turned them over to what is known as a reprobate state of mind. To become reprobate means:

* To be rejected by God; cast off as worthless.
* Immoral, having no religious or principled character.

This is dangerous because in this state, one becomes "numb" to what is true and what is right, because they have determined to satisfy their own desires. Take heed, for when this becomes God's resolve, it means He has made the decision to no longer strive with the one who refuses to listen and obey, according to Genesis 6:3. Also know this: whatever He tells you to let go of, it is so that He can uproot all the residue of everything that is connected to what He delivered you from, to rebuild you for the new life He has for you. Rest assured that God will fill every void and every lonely place, and reveal truths like never before.

When there is an undeniable press in your spirit to turn from something, take heed because God is speaking. There are many whom God has been dealing with for years about making this decision, but now is the time to choose to obey God. Jesus Christ is soon to return, and He is coming for His bride, the Church: a church without spot or wrinkle or any such blemish (Ephesians 5:27). This is why there is such a war in the spirit surrounding this topic, but God is using His people who have obeyed to speak on His behalf and sound the alarm.

In the previous chapter, I spoke briefly about separation, and it is vitally important that those who identify as blood-washed believers of Jesus Christ acknowledge the necessity of the call to separation that God is requiring. Understand the significance of the definition of the word separation: "the act of disuniting two or more things, or the condition of being separated."

Let's gain even more insight by defining what it means to disunite: "to separate, sever, or split."

It is a matter of refraining from mixing the holy with the unholy; the clean with the unclean, and God makes it very clear throughout the Bible that He is absolutely against it. The Spirit of God reminded me of what took place when Nebuchadnezzar took over as king of Jerusalem. Pay close attention to what is described in Daniel 1:1-2 when he invaded Judah:

"In the third year of the reign of Jehoiakim king of Judah, came Nebuchadnezzar king of Babylon unto Jerusalem, and besieged it. And the Lord gave Jehoiakim king of Judah into his hand, with part of the vessels of the house of God, which he carried into the land of Shinar to the house of his god; and he brought the vessels into the treasure house of his god."

God began to give me understanding of why He led me to this scripture: it begins with three significant words in these two passages: vessels, God, and god. By definition, a vessel can be in two forms:

1. A container of liquid or other substance, such as glass, goblet, cup, bottle, bowl, or pitcher,

2. A person as a container of qualities or feelings.

We understand that there is only one true and living God the Father, and therefore we show Him reverence by capitalizing His name as God. The Word makes plain that false idols are identified as gods with lowercase letters. Some of you may say, "I no longer take part in any of the rituals during chapter meetings or conventions; I only sit in on the sessions where business is being conducted and voting is taking place on key matters." There are those who might say, "I don't wear any paraphernalia that displays the organization, but I am an active member who works hard within the organization."

Others may say, "I haven't been active in the organization in years, so this doesn't pertain to me." What does this have to do with membership in these organizations?

Nebuchadnezzar was a wicked king who, when he invaded Jerusalem, began to implement his wicked beliefs and practices. He took the holy vessels from the house of God and mixed them in an unholy place where idol worship took place. For this reason, the wrath of God came upon Nebuchadnezzar.

If we profess to be vessels of honor in Christ Jesus, we have no right to take what is supposed to be presented "holy and acceptable" unto God our Father and mix it with that which is associated with unholy idol gods. For those who profess to be blood-washed believers and followers of Jesus Christ, this is what sanctification is all about:

Sanctification – the process of making holy; hallowing, consecration.

Here's an analogy to consider: in the natural, if I wash and sanitize a load of clothes, put them in the dryer, and add scented dryer sheets, when they are done drying, they should come out looking renewed and smelling fresh because they have gone through a cleaning process. If I then take the clothes that have just gone through a thorough cleaning process and mix them back in with clothes that have stains and odors that now rub off onto the clean clothes, they are now tainted and have to be rewashed.

This is what it is likened to in the spirit: when we are called to sanctify ourselves, we must separate from everything that conflicts with a lifestyle that is holy unto God and threatens to restain us with the old sin nature. We must also be careful not to take on a spirit of haughtiness that causes one to believe that seniority in age, title, position, or so-called "ranking" makes it impossible for you to need correction or have truth revealed. God has the power and authority to use whomever He chooses to deliver a message in an effort to see His purpose carried out, as recorded in John 3:16, because He loves us and wishes that no one would perish (2 Peter 3:9).

As Paul repeatedly stressed to the seven churches in Asia to whom he was charged with delivering the word of the Lord, "He who hath an ear, let him hear what the Spirit saith to the churches."

Those who truly walk in the Spirit operate in humility; it is through humility that we allow our spiritual ears to hear what the Spirit of God is saying and take heed. Walking in humility causes one to shun the very appearance of pride and arrogance because the contrite posture of our heart seeks to please God. The years spent being committed to any man-made thing mean nothing to God, and don't fare in comparison when He requires us to obey His instructions.

I also realize that, regardless of the reference to Christian beliefs being the foundation of these organizations, not everyone who decides to read this book may profess to be a Christian. As someone who also serves in ministry leadership alongside my husband, I am even more sensitive to the call of reaching souls as the Lord leads. My hope is that the seeds of the word planted through this book will produce a harvest for the saving and sanctifying of your soul.

If no one has ever extended an invitation to you, or if you are in a backslidden state, I invite you to receive Jesus Christ as Lord and Savior over your life. As long as you have breath in your body, it's not too late to change your course and let God set your feet on the path that leads to righteousness and truth. Scripture tells us that our obedience is better than sacrifice (1 Samuel 15:22): this means that making the decision to obey God and let go of the things that can jeopardize the eternal residency of our soul is far more important than what we feel like we are losing in this present life.

I urge you to ask God to give you the strength and courage to hear, acknowledge, accept, and obey His truth. Don't allow the ungodly counsel of the flesh (yours or anyone else's) to persuade you that God is not speaking through what is written in the pages of this book.

GLOSSARY OF TERMS

1. **Greek Life** – the reference to being a part of any organization that is identified by specific Greek letters.

2. **Secret society** – an organization that conceals its activities, events, membership, or inner workings, and may or may not try to hide its existence.

3. **Elite Eight** – a previous reference to the existence of the black greek letter fraternities and sororities, prior to the addition of Iota Phi Theta Fraternity.

4. **Divine Nine** – the current reference to the existence of the black greek letter fraternities and sororities.

5. **Rush** – an event sponsored by a sorority, where perspective women who are interested in membership come to learn more about the organization.

6. **Smoker** – an event sponsored by a fraternity, where perspective men who are interested in membership come to learn more about the organization.

7. **Paper** – a derogatory term that suggests that someone did not earn their membership by going through underground pledging activities.

8. **Spirit man** – the inward part of man's being.

9. **Rhema word** – a spiritual communication or inspiration from God.

10. **Soul tie** - A metaphysical connection between a person and someone or something else, formed by being extremely close to them.

11. **Dean of Pledges** - one who is responsible for a line of pledges and oversees the pledge process.

12. **Neophyte** – a new member of a sorority or fraternity.